The Murder of Jeanne Clery

Pete Dove

Published by Trellis Publishing, 2021.

THE MURDER OF JEANNE CLERY

First edition. July 7, 2021.

Copyright © 2021 Pete Dove.

ISBN: 979-8224521036

Written by Pete Dove.

THE MURDER OF JEANNE CLERY

PETE DOVE

When Good Comes from Bad

To discover that our daughter has been raped and murdered. Such horror is unthinkable. Lives changed forever. Pain every single day. To find out that this has happened in a place where she should have been safe surely makes the agony worse. If that is possible. Very little offers balm to that level of suffering.

Maybe though, just maybe, ensuring that our loved one did not die in vain can help, even if in the most fractional sense. The hurt, guilt, physical pain in the heart and head all remain. Every day continues to be a battle. Mental health still wavers between deep, deep depression and uncontrollable anger. Plus, every emotion in between. But there is some good to emerge, slithering, creeping, sliding out of those dark, weeping caverns of our distress.

Of course, falling victim to a rapist is a very unusual occurrence. Being murdered by them as well is even more unlikely to happen. We read about such vile tragedies every day, and it can seem as though the world is an unthinkably dangerous place for our children, even when they have grown up. It is not. There are around one hundred and sixty-five million women living in the US, and approximately four hundred thousand will report falling victim to a sexual assault of some kind or other each year. The figure is unsurprisingly much lower for men.

That is still one woman in four hundred falling prey to a molester every year. Too many. The percentage was much higher in 1980 – in fact, it has fallen by around eighty per cent since those days. A part of the reason for that is the work undertaken by the parents of Jeanne Cleary. When Jeanne died, aged just nineteen, during her freshman year at university, her mourning parents decided to do something. To make a difference, in their daughter's name. That difference was needed, because although the overall percentage of people who are subject to sexual attack is low, an inordinately high number of victims come from the student body. More than one in eight students, it is estimated by the Rape, Abuse and Incest National Network, experience some form of sexual attack during their academic lives. With nearly 20 million students in the US, that is almost two and a half million young people in total. Now that really is too many. Clearly, these figures do not match up with the ones in the previous paragraph, which indicates how many such attacks go unreported.

Jeanne was born to Howard and Connie Clery on November 23rd, 1966. She was their youngest child. Her big brothers were Howard III and Benjamin. The siblings grew up in Bryn Mawr, where her mother still resides. This unusual name comes from the Welsh word for 'big hill'. The area was settled by a Welshman who escaped religious persecution in Britain in the eighteenth century. The small region of only just over half a square mile sits close to the border with Delaware, creeping beyond it in places, although Jeanne and her family lived over in the Pennsylvania side. It was a comfortable place to have a childhood, with lots of young families and plenty of work and jobs. Her parents were well enough off to give Jeanne and her siblings a promising future. Although Howard had suffered from polio as a teenager and spent the rest of his life requiring a steel leg brace and canes to get around, he was a successful business man, firstly working for Gillette Co in Boston and later going on to become an executive with a number of companies, including with Raytheon Co, a technological company, and Royal McBee, which gained a name for its production of typewriters. He also purchased a printing business, which he turned into a hugely successful national direct-mail company. By 1987, a year after Jeanne's death, the business was reporting sales figures of more than $40 million. However, by 1991, Howard was committing himself fully to being an activist for improved university and college campus security. Howard and Connie were driven, and successful. If anybody was going to create a window of transparency on a shameful secret of American education, it was going to be people such as them.

Connie and Howard, who died from a heart attack on 1st January 2008, were typically caring parents. Lehigh did not hold a great reputation for campus security. But neither they nor their daughter knew this. If they had, most probably she would have attended a different University, they explained later. They went on to sue Lehigh University, stating that had they known that their youngest daughter was attending an institution with a reputation for 'slipshod' campus security, where thirty-eight assaults and other violent crimes had taken place in the three years leading up to their daughter's death, they and she would have behaved differently. Certainly, even had Jeanne decided to attend Lehigh, she would have been much more careful about her own personal safety.

Jeanne's death was brutal and merciless. Fellow student Josoph Henry found his way into her room and was robbing it when she woke and surprised him. Out of his mind on alcohol and marijuana, Henry went mad. He cut and beat the blond haired, attractive nineteen-year-old. Then he raped and sodomised her, before finally strangling her to death. Henry had entered her room because, as was an unsafe but far from unusual practice at Stoughton Hall at the University, Jeanne's door had been propped open. Auto locking doors were fitted in the dorms, but there had been over 180 cases of these being bypassed by the residents themselves. These young people were simply not aware of the dangers of this practice, and the University was doing nothing to disabuse them of their notion that their actions were safe.

In Jeanne's case, the door was propped open because her roommate was out and had not taken her key with her. Young people do not see danger; that is a sad fact of life.

On the face of it, as strange as such a statement might seem, Josoph Henry was not a bad man. At least, when he was sober. He had a fondness for marijuana, but that is not especially unusual among the young, especially back in the mid-1980s. He also enjoyed consuming quantities of alcohol. According to Henry himself, it was this particular drug which changed his character during a weekend visit from his younger brother at the time of the freshmen weekend at Lehigh University in April 1986.

But Henry knew that alcohol had a bad effect on him. Even when, as on the day of his crime, he was high on Marijuana as well. His usually calm demeanour changed when he fell under its influence. At least, that is the story purported by the man, now in his fifties and serving a life sentence at the State Correctional Institution at Dallas, Pennsylvania. It was not an excuse found acceptable by the court.

The weekend in question at Lehigh University was not unusual. There was some theatrical drama to enjoy, a game of basketball. Parties. Nothing strange with regards to student life. Henry claims that he smoked marijuana to heighten his enjoyment of the weekend – he would have consumed more, instead of the alcohol had some been available. The drug 'did not cause any kind of violent reactions,' he said, which was not the case when he consumed alcohol. It seems as though he drank a lot, because at some point he smashed down a door at a party he was attending. His friends saw him losing control and took him for a drive in the hope that this would calm him down. It didn't. Next, he wandered around the campus, and discovered a door unlocked and propped open. It led to a dormitory. There Henry spotted a man who was sleeping on a couch. Although the guy was unknown to the drunken student, and had certainly done him no harm, Henry claims that the sight of him triggered some sort of violent reaction.

'I had this thought to just hurt this person,' he said many years later, speaking to a different University paper. 'This guy just sleeping on the couch. It was the first, really, the violent thought that got everything started. The guy sleeping on the couch.'

But the thought did not result in actions, yet. Instead, he chose to continue his wander around the campus. Open door followed open door. Security was notable by its absence. But then, it was a party weekend. They were on campus. These young adults, barely more than kids, were safe. Weren't they? They had little reason to suspect otherwise.

'Found an open door,' continued Henry, 'I opened one door, there was a bunch of people sleeping there. I remember that. Opened another door, there was Jeanne Clery, who I didn't know at the time. Asleep. Entered the room and, uuh.'

The charge sheet presented against Henry was long and unpleasant. Murder in the first degree. Rape. Involuntary deviant sexual intercourse. Indecent assault. It continues. Burglary, theft, robbery and aggravated assault. It took a little over a year from the date of his attack for Henry's case to come to court. The jury found him guilty on each of the above accounts. His defence that he had committed the crime under the influence of alcohol, and therefore his judgement was significantly lacking, enough to mitigate his guilt, was rejected. However, the court did accept that he was drunk, just that this could not be used in his defence. Notes from the case explained why: 'The law has developed in Pennsylvania that a defendant cannot...be insulated from criminal liability in his actions by claiming a mental state resulting from alcohol which was voluntarily ingested. Whether or not appellant was aware that he we would suffer from the mental state is irrelevant. The fact that he voluntarily ingested the alcohol being determinative in depriving him of an insanity defense.' There we have it. Getting yourself drunk is no defense against any crimes you subsequently commit.

Later, Henry accepted this his crime was abominable. 'If I had known drunkenness could cause me to do what I did, I would not have gotten drunk,' he said. However, his contention that he was also emotionally hurt and angry when he committed the crime was not really borne out by either the fun weekend he had enjoyed with his younger brother, nor the comments from his mother. Marie Henry continues to suffer her own guilt and sadness at the effective loss of her son, along with the knowledge of what he did to cause her that loss. 'I thought we had a great family connection,' she said later. 'That we did everything together, and that we went places and we would talk to each other and we would have those family times.' She speaks to her son daily by phone, and visits him once a month, a four hour round trip.

Henry says that he recognises his guilt, and now spends his time working to raise the dangers of alcohol on young people. He remains a practising Christian, supporting younger inmates and belonging to a bible study group. He writes for a prison mentoring website and contributes to a devotional guide.

Whilst he knows he will most likely die in prison, he tries daily to improve his life. His long-term future, though, is a worry to his mother. Understandably. She knows she will not be around forever, and the only other family member is Jason, the younger brother, who has not been able to bring himself to visit Josoph in prison. Indeed, Henry was originally sentenced to death by electric chair. As in most capital decisions, he appealed but the verdict and sentence were initially upheld by the Pennsylvania Supreme Court. However, in 2002 the sentence was overturned, albeit not permanently. At that stage, Henry agreed to give up any further rights of appeal and accept a life sentence rather than face the possibility that the courts could reinstate his death sentence.

Henry was caught quickly following the crime. He confessed the murder to some friends, and they in turn reported the matter to police. So, there was no dramatic and long-lasting search, false accusations or fears among the student body that a serial killer was at loose. Not that this changed the fact that the university had failed to keep students aware of risks of living on a campus with numerous other people. They could argue that they had done their bit by fitting the self-locking doors, but this holds little water. Fitting a fire safety system is no good if the water supply to the sprinklers is turned off, and nobody is told of the danger of lighting a fire in a room. Nor did the quick arrest do little to ease the pain suffered by Connie and Howard, their sons or Jeanne's friends and wider family.

Lastly, Henry claims to recognise the damage and irreparable hurt his actions caused. 'What I should've told my victim's family,' he says, 'is that my heart is broken due to the evil of my crime and broken by the pain I caused them. I should've pledged my continued prayers for them to experience God's peace. God's comfort, and the healing that only God can give.'

Whether this is something Connie can accept, or Howard could have taken in while he was still alive, is hard to determine. They are clearly proactive people, and the hurt Henry caused drove them on to do something very worthwhile, and extremely beneficial. The extent to which their passion could also lead them on to forgiveness is another matter entirely. Following Jeanne's death, they lobbied as hard as they could to force Government to enact legislation which might have saved their daughter's life. To make universities and colleges publicise information about their security, their attitude towards their students' safety, and the actual incidents of crime that happened on their campus.

The pressure worked, and in 1990 President George H. W. Bush signed the paperwork. The Clery Act became law. Type the words into a search engine nowadays and lists of Universities appear, with each heading directing searchers to their own Clery Act report. Parents and students can find out easily how safe their child's continuing education is likely to be. No longer is such important information hidden under a veil of secrecy, like dirty washing from the eyes of neighbours.

'When your daughter is slaughtered,' said Howard in 1990, you have two choices – curl up and let the world go by or fight back.' He went on to contend that by not slipping into an understandable state or depressed torpor he and his wife were, in their daughter's name, 'helping others but also ourselves.'

So, what does the Clery Act look like? It requires both universities and colleges to adhere to a number of conditions. Any institution of this kind must report annually to both employees and students. On October 1st each year it must make public an annual security report, known as an ASR. This document must include statistics covering crimes that have occurred on the campus over the previous three calendar years. It must also indicate what actions have been undertaken to improve safety on the site.

A number of policy statements should appear on the report. These include, amongst others, reports on crimes that have occurred, the security provided on the campus, and how it is accessed. There is little point in employing measures if they sit in a portable cabin all day, hidden away out of sight of visitors and residents alike. There must be a policy statement on law enforcement authority as well.

Then the requirements become even more relevant and hard hitting. It might seem so far as though the Cleary Act is little more than a bureaucratic exercise for ticking boxes and covering backs. But it is not. It is a real measure that helps to protect people – students, employees and visitors. No institution wishes to have a reputation for putting those under its care at risk. And, with the best will in the world, organisations will twist the truth to their own ends. A cold list of crimes that have occurred can be spun or explained away. But the following list of policy statements really does get to the heart of young persons' safety.

The Cleary Act requires universities and colleges to record their response to the use of alcohol and drugs. It requires them to state their procedures towards the prevention of sexual assault. It charges them with providing clearly and unambiguously their response to the following four areas of crime. Firstly, once again sexual assault. But it does not stop of this. It is well known that sexual predators build up to their crimes through lesser, although still frightening and potentially dangerous activities. So, the Act also states that institutions must state their policy regarding domestic abuse. It goes further still, specifically including a mention of dating violence. It adds stalking to the list of crimes about which the ASR must be explicit.

The effectiveness of such legislature is apparent. Universities and colleges are competitive places. The service they provide might be academic and educational, but they still need customers – students – in order to thrive. Or even survive. Where their response to campus crime is inadequate this becomes apparent in three ways. Firstly, in the number of crimes that have actually occurred in recent years. Secondly in the quality of their response to these. And perhaps most significantly in these clear statements of their policies towards such illegalities.

It is easy, we might argue, to write a policy statement. Easier still to stretch it, twist it and, if it is more convenient to do so, ignore it. But the annual report brings all of these aspects of dealing with campus crime together, and in doing so it is clear if a university or a college is not doing enough to protect those who use it, either to learn or to teach.

Simply, no parent is going to send their children off to an institution where they will not be safe, in the process paying thousands upon thousands of dollars to do so. A place that is not safe, or does not have a positive and proactive approach to safety, or – worst of all – is disingenuous regarding what they state are their policies, will find its student numbers falling. The best staff will leave, because they know the truth, and will wish to secure their own careers in an organisation which acts with propriety. The result is that student numbers will fall further, and that college or university will – rightly enough – be no more.

But there is much more still. Alongside sexual crime matters, other offences which must be recorded and made public include murder, including manslaughter and, tellingly for educational institutions manslaughter by negligence. Robbery and burglary must be included, as should physical assaults, motor thefts and arson.

Hate crime levels must be reported, and a policy statement regarding them issued. Included in this category, alongside more serious assaults are intimidation and vandalism. A young person should be able to undertake their higher education free from the threat of discrimination. The Cleary Act helps to ensure that they can do so.

Violations regarding weapons must also be reported.

The Act is not just retrospective. It also requires universities and colleges to issue what it calls 'timely warnings' of threats to students or employees. To fulfil this requirement of the act it must look more widely than the campus itself, and include information about crimes that have happened nearby, and might therefore present a threat to those living on the campus, working there, learning at the institution and travelling into and away from it. Once again, a policy statement regarding its approach to issuing timely warnings must appear on the institutions' annual security report.

The Act certainly pressurises organisations to conform to its requirements. We have seen above how reputational damage, fatal in extreme cases, might occur if one does not. But there are further levels of scrutiny. Compliance with the act is overseen by the United States Department of Education. It can, and does, impose significant fines – up to more than $50,000 per individual infringement of the requirements – for shortfalls and breaches. It can also suspend an institution from participation in federal student financial programmes. Such a punishment could effectively close an institution down.

The Cleary Act has teeth, and a number of institutions have faced the financial and reputational handicap of being found in non-compliance with its requirements. Pennsylvania State University, Eastern Michigan University, Virginia Tech and the University of Montana have all discovered to their cost that the overseeing authority are prepared to take action if they fall short in their duties to students and employees with regards to safety.

Pennsylvania State University faced a fine of nearly two and a half million dollars in relation to its alleged failure to report allegations of sex offences against its former coach Jerry Sandusky. At the Eastern Michigan University was fined of over three hundred and fifty thousand dollars over the way it reacted when a student was assaulted and killed in 2006. Although the university did report the incident, it failed to issue appropriate timely warnings, and information given regarding the attack was judged to be inadequate. Although the fine was small compared to some other breaches at other institutions, the punishment was considered significant because of the message it sent to America's universities and colleges.

Clearly, the fine stated, institutions must act fully in line with the letter of the law, and its spirits. Boards took note, and the Act began to become ever more effective. However, East Michigan University's failure to meet its duty cost its president his job.

Virginia Tech was issued with a fine following the massacre there in 2007. It was also given a fine for its failure to give a timely warning after the shootings. However, it appealed and the US Department of Education agreed with its arguments, the law judge stating: 'This (the time the warning was finally given) was not an unreasonable amount of time in which to issue a warning. If the later shootings at Norris Hall had not occurred, it is doubtful that the timing of the email would have been perceived as too late.'

Michigan State University was not as fortunate. Lawrence, known as Larry, Nasser was on the face of it the sort of upstanding individual parents would be proud to have looking after their child. He was the USA Gymnastics team doctor and an osteopathic physician. He was also a professor at the Michigan State University College of Human Medicine. Unfortunately, there was another line on Nasser's resume. One he would rather not include. He was also a serial rapist and sex offender, who preyed on the young. Among his victims was an Olympic gold medallist, McKayla Maroney, whom he began to molest when she was just thirteen years old.

It seems as though those in charge at Michigan State had an inkling as to what their professor was up to and decided that it was best to look away rather than take action. The university paid for its negligent attitude with a fine from the US Department of Education of four and a half million dollars. That was on top of numerous law suits it faced from complainants.

Other institutions, including University of California Berkeley, have fallen foul of the act. Berkeley was given a hefty fine and subject to a monitoring condition following administrative and policy failures. The Act genuinely is delivering results and making institutions safer.

Had Jeanne Cleary, and her parents, had greater insight into safety on campus at Lehigh University, they might have chosen a different institution. Jeanne may have been alive today. She is not, but thousands of other young and older people have seen their own education delivered more safely, their own careers carried out in secure institutions. Jeanne's death, as little comfort as this is to her friends, her family and her mother, really has made life safer for others. A plaque can be found outside of Stoughton Hall at the Lehigh University. 'Lest we forget the meaning of her death, that we must protect one another, so that her life will not have been in vain,' it states, each word capitalised.

All can be assured, the Clery Act ensures that her young life was not given for nothing

.

THE MURDER OF FAITH HEDGEPETH

JESSI DAVIS

Happy-go-lucky

In 1982, Connie Hedgepeth had her hands full with two teenage daughters and a husband who was addicted to drugs. Her marriage was struggling when she took a pregnancy test, hoping the result would be negative. It wasn't. Her youngest daughter was born eight months later, and Connie named her Faith.

"I felt like it was my faith in God that helped me through that situation," she said. "My faith helped me to continue to work and to do what I needed to do for my children."

Still, Connie divorced her husband when Faith was still young. Struggling to stay afloat, Connie turned to her oldest daughter, Rolanda, for support. Despite an almost 18-year age difference, Rolanda and Faith developed a strong bond – "part mother-daughter, part sister," Rolanda explained.

"We were always close. I was kind of like a second mom, but there was that sister bond, too," she said.

Rolanda's daughter Alexis was born on Faith's first birthday, and the two girls grew up together in rural North Carolina. Her upbringing was difficult, but Faith's positive attitude and eagerness to contribute propelled her through her schooling. She was an honor student, a cheerleader, and a regular volunteer for many other clubs and organizations.

"She always had this energy about her," Rolanda recalled. "She was really happy-go-lucky."

Faith's father had dropped out of college to raise his family, and Faith intended to pick up where her dad had left off. She earned a Gates Millennium Scholarship to the University of North Carolina at Chapel Hill – the very school her father had been attending. Poised to be the very first college graduate in her family, Faith had plans to become a pediatrician or a teacher once she completed her education.

Instead, the Native American biology major never made it to her 20th birthday. Police records reveal that Faith was last seen alive at approximately 3 a.m. on September 7, 2012, when she and her roommate Karena Rosario came home after an evening partying at a local nightclub.

The Thrill of a lifetime

The night before she was murdered, Faith had been studying with Karena at the Davis Library, on the university campus. At around 8 or 8:30 p.m., Faith took a break from her studies to send a text to her father – "Hey Daddy, I love you," the message read. She also texted her niece, reminding her to register to vote in the upcoming election.

At around midnight, the girls left the library and stopped back at their apartment before heading out at approximately 1 a.m. to arrive at a nightclub called The Thrill.

Just after 2:30 a.m., the girls left the bar. Karena was feeling sick after having had too much to drink, and wanted to go home. Faith helped Karena get into bed, and then fell asleep herself. However, a text message from Faith's phone was received at 3:40 a.m. by Brandon Edwards, Karena's ex-boyfriend.

"Hey b. can you come over here please," the message read. "Karena needs you more aha. You know. Please let her know you care."

A few minutes later, another text comes through that simply says, "than." It is suspected that the message was intended to fix a typo in the original message, correcting it to say "Karena needs you more *than* you know." Brandon didn't reply until the next day, when Faith's phone received a text at 4:16 p.m. that read, "Who is this?"

At around 4:30 a.m., Karena left the apartment to go over to a friend's house – and claims that she did see Faith asleep at that time. When she returned at around 11 a.m., however, she found her roommate's body in her room, in her bed, "covered by a blanket on top of her slightly askew mattress with large amounts of blood."

At 11:01 a.m., a 911 call came from the house.

Faith was unconscious and cold, Karena told the dispatcher who took the call, and there was "blood everywhere." She said she thought there may have been an altercation, explaining to the dispatcher that "there were items in the room that were not hers and that it looked like someone else had been there."

Police responded immediately, securing the scene at the girls' apartment complex and collecting evidence. They found Faith's body "positioned on the floor, leaning against the bed, with her shirt pulled up and no clothes from the waist down."

Medical examiners concluded that the cause of death was blunt force trauma, based on the severe beating Faith had endured. When the autopsy report was unsealed nearly two years after the killing, it was revealed that she also had bruises and cuts all over her arms and legs, as well as blood underneath her fingernails.

"It's very, very hard, learning of how Faith died," said Rolanda. "She was beaten, she was bludgeoned to death. A lot of people don't understand what that means, but it was really bad."

A rape kit had also been performed, indicating the presence of semen – with DNA that matched other DNA that police had recovered at the scene. Law enforcement officials have not confirmed whether the sexual activity was consensual or forced.

Searching for suspects

In the years since Faith's death, multiple search warrants have been executed – as well as numerous court orders for things like cell phones, computers, and even social media accounts. DNA testing has also been carried out on many of men that interacted with Karena and Faith while they were at the nightclub, but so far, investigators have found no matching results.

While at The Thrill, Faith was reportedly dancing with a man named David Bell. He told police he didn't know Faith very well, and was not named by police as a suspect during the investigation.

"(Redacted) was identified as walking out of Club Thrill with Faith Hedgepeth shortly before the homicide occurred," read a police report unsealed in 2014. "He was the last male to be seen with her before her death."

The report added that Bell admitted to talking with Faith the night she was killed, and to meeting her the weekend before. He refused to provide investigators with a sample of his DNA, claiming that he had likely touched her at some point during the night of the homicide. His statements to law enforcement officers were also determined to be "inconsistent" with statements provided by others.

Another man, Jacob Beatley, was interviewed by police and also not named as a suspect. Karena visited him during the early morning hours of September 7, after leaving the apartment she shared with Faith. DNA was also sought from a man named Reginald Leonard Jackson II, who was not named as a suspect despite having been texting regularly with Faith in the days prior to her murder.

However, none of this information was offered to Faith's family until the documents were unsealed in 2014.

"All they have said to us and to the public, to the media, to everybody, (is) that this wasn't random – how do they know that?" said Chad Hedgepeth, Faith's brother. "Do they have a suspect? Do they have any suspects? ... Tell us something, because being in the dark on any and everything these past four weeks has been brutal."

While the recording from the 911 call seems to indicate that Karena was alone when she discovered Faith's body in their apartment, the police report stated that she returned to their home with a friend. In the recording, however, Karena consistently claims "I just walked into my apartment," instead of saying "we." There is also no sound recorded that could be attributed to another person in the room.

An analysis of the call could suggest that the repetition of the statement "I just walked into my apartment" is an attempt to establish an alibi – especially since the recording reveals that Karena says this several times before even providing the dispatcher with necessary information like the victim's state or the location of the emergency.

At no point in the call does Karena specifically ask for help for the victim. She also apologizes to the dispatcher, using language that analysts typically see in calls where guilty knowledge is indicated.

Initially, law enforcement turned their attention to Eriq Takoy Jones – an ex-boyfriend of Karena's who lived in the same apartment complex and was reportedly an aspiring rapper. Just a few months before the murder, Karena had filed a restraining order against Eriq, on the basis of domestic assault. Police had previously investigated claims that Eriq had kicked two of the doors in the girls' apartment completely off their frames, and eyewitness accounts reported that Karena had been seen with visible injuries to her body – inflicted, she said, by her ex-boyfriend.

"Faith took Karena to take out a restraining order," said Faith's father, Roland Hedgepeth. "I think that very possibly, Takoy may have had some ill feelings toward Faith for doing that."

Rolanda said Faith had moved in with Karena after the restraining order had been filed, to help her friend as she recovered from the abusive relationship.

"I wasn't worried about Faith at the time," Rolanda said. "I wanted them to be safe. I just wanted both of them to be safe."

Just before Faith was murdered, Eriq posted a chilling message on his Facebook page, and texted a similar message to an acquaintance.

"Deal Lord," the post read. "Forgive me for all of my sins and the sins I may commit today. Protect me from the girls who don't deserve me and the ones who wish me dead today."

An unnamed person who claimed to be a former roommate of Faith's called the Chapel Hill Police Department the day after Faith's body was discovered with additional concerning information about Eriq. According to the caller, Faith had told her that Karena's boyfriend hated her (Faith) and told her that if Karena wouldn't get back together with him, he would kill Faith.

However, Eriq was very cooperative with law enforcement during the investigation into Faith's murder. Both his apartment and car were combed for trace evidence, and his DNA was tested and cleared.

"From what I knew of her (Faith), she was the sweetest person in the world. If you needed her and she could do it, she was there," Eriq told news reporters after Faith's murder. "I'll be honest with you – whoever did this deserves to burn."

Investigators also learned that the ex-boyfriend of Karena's that Faith had texted in the hours before she was killed had also been present that night at The Thrill. Police records indicated that Brandon Edwards had even spent the night at the girls' apartment the night before the murder – making his response to Faith's texts the day she was killed quite unusual.

According to a friend named Marisol Rangel, Karena and Brandon were "just friends" at the time of Faith's murder. Marisol is the friend who was reportedly with Karena when she discovered Faith's body, but the 911 operator was confident that Karena was alone when the call was placed.

In January 2013, police released a profile of the killer. According to the profile, developed by Chapel Hill Police and the FBI's Behavioral Analysis Unit, the person responsible for Faith's murder might have been familiar with her – and possibly even lived near her in the past.

The individual may have also "made comments" about Faith in the past, with their behavior shifting after the murder occurred. Obviously, the profile indicated this person would have been "unaccounted for" during the early morning hours of September 7, 2012. Police also stated the DNA evidence collected at the scene of the homicide points toward a "male suspect."

At the time, Faith's father Roland said the development of the profile marked a "new beginning" in the investigation, and believed it would help police solve the case.

"For us, we're kind of stuck back on September 7," he said. "Every day, we get up and relive that day. But I'm confident things will open up soon."

Strange evidence

Nearly two years after the murder, police released a shocking and mysterious piece of evidence. A spiteful, handwritten note was found scrawled on a fast food bag left near the crime scene, with the words "I'M NOT STUPID BITCH JEALOUS."

Police believe the note was written by the killer, but have not said whether the handwriting has ever been officially analyzed. According to private investigator and forensic handwriting examiner Peggy Walla, some clues can be determined from the note.

"What struck me was how clean the document is – the crime scene was pretty bloody, and there's nothing on this document," she said. "Looking at it, I would get the impression it was either written outside of the crime scene, or it was written before, like a premeditation."

She also feels the words were written by a non-dominant hand, indicating that whoever wrote the note was attempting to "disguise" their penmanship. The block letters could be taken as the writer's attempt to distance themselves from authority, she said.

"The word and sentence phrase 'I'm not stupid' is a hot push-button factor," Walla added. "That's probably the most important thing said. This was a jealous person who was called 'stupid.' The person that said it who is now deceased has no way of repeating this person is stupid, which is another way to shut them up."

Users of online forums have also speculated that the use of the word 'jealous' could indicate that the writer of the note was a woman, as the word is thought to be more frequently used by females. The formation of the letter 'P' in particular has also struck some as seeming feminine in nature.

Other speculation surrounds the intent of the note. The words 'jealous' and 'bitch' suggest that the note was not meant for the police of for the public – rather, these deeply personal words were likely intended toward Faith, or possibly even Karena, who would eventually find the body. But more curious yet is the situation that must have occurred that led to the writing of the note. What happened before Faith was murdered?

Cries for help

A clue may be found in a voicemail left for a friend the night of her death. The call appears to have been a pocket-dial – a very timely pocket-dial that potentially recorded the final minutes of Faith's life. The timestamp on the nearly unintelligible message indicates that the call was made while Faith was still at The Thrill, but some have argued that a glitch in technology could have resulted in an incorrect time.

According to President and CEO of Creative Forensic Services Arlo West, who is certified by the New York Institute of Forensic Audio in enhancement, authentication, and analysis of both audio and video, the names 'Rosie' and 'Eriq' appear throughout the recording – potentially referring to Karena Rosario and her ex-boyfriend Eriq Takoy Jones.

"I've worked on hundreds, if not thousands, of cases where people have pocket-dialed somebody," West said. "If you can peel back those layers of noise, you start to get a better picture of the dialogue that is contained – stuff that starts to make a little more sense."

In his analysis for Crime Watch Daily, West identified two distinct female voices – one which he claimed is Faith Hedgepeth, and the other he describes as a "very angry female." He also picked out at least two male voices.

"I hear what I believe is Miss Hedgepeth's cries for help," West said. "You can hear her emotive voice, the tone of her voice, is clearly in pain ... You can clearly hear what I believe is Faith pleading. She's being hurt, being attacked."

West said he feels "very confident" about hearing the names 'Rosie' and 'Eriq,' and included both names in his transcript of the three-minute recording.

He also claims iPhones were "inherently problematic with timestamping" during the time Faith was killed – which he said accounts for the timestamp on the voicemail showing 1:23 a.m., while police believe Faith was killed sometime after 4:30 a.m. Still, Chapel Hill police did contact West for an official analysis of the recording.

"If it is Faith being murdered, and captured in this recording – which I think it is, this is pivotal," West said. "It should be able to solve this case."

Police seem to believe that the voicemail was recorded from the club, not from the apartment – and in the middle of the call, there appears to be music playing or someone rapping. There is also no evidence to support that the name 'Rosie' could have referred to Karena, and Eriq Takoy Jones was apparently called 'Takoy' by his friends.

Still, the voicemail is difficult to discount – especially since, on the night Faith was murdered, it appears to have recorded an emotionally-charged, angry discussion. To many listeners, including members of Faith's family, the voices sound agitated – belligerent, fast-speaking – and seem to be punctuated by audible yelps of what could be pain.

"From day one, I heard my daughter screaming in the background," said Faith's father, Roland. "I knew something was going on."

"A really good case."

The note, the voicemail audio, and other documents – including the 15-page autopsy – were unsealed in September 2014. According to Chris Blue, Chapel Hill Police Chief, the effort was an attempt to generate new leads in the investigation.

"We have excellent evidence – we have a really good case," he said. "We just need to connect this really good case with the killer."

However, in those two years, police had been unable to connect any potential suspect with the crime. The official documents were sealed during that time despite repeated requests from lawyers and news organizations to open them to the public, as investigators felt releasing the information would compromise their efforts.

"It's not that it might hinder this investigation, it will hinder this investigation," said Durham County Assistant District Attorney Charlene Franks.

She added that details contained within the documents, including the 911 call where the crime scene and body are vividly described, could help police identify the killer – as that information would have been known by very few people.

In a "cold case," Franks said, police will often turn to the public for assistance. However, since the investigation into Faith's murder is ongoing, solving the case means keeping the public – including Faith's family – in the dark about some vital details.

"The most important thing to them and the state and the Chapel Hill Police Department is to find the killer of their baby girl, Faith Hedgepeth," she said. "The only way to do that is to keep those items sealed because the information contained in there, other than (investigators), only the killer knows."

According to Steve Hale, private investigator and retired homicide detective who was never involved with the case, it's typical for law enforcement to keep the details of a case under wraps – interviews and tips that haven't been influenced by media reports can make or break a case.

"If there is a suspect, he may not know he's a suspect, and they're waiting for him to get careless and maybe make a comment to an accessory after the fact," he said, adding that detectives likely suspected someone who knew Faith and might have had a distinct motive.

Each document pertaining to the case was reviewed by Judge Howard Manning before being unsealed in 2014. Still, three investigators with the Chapel Hill Police Department and State Bureau of Investigation continued working exclusively on the unsolved case – and offered a reward of $40,000 for any information leading to the arrest and conviction of Faith's killer.

"We really want to bring some peace to Faith's family," said Blue. "This has been two unimaginable years for them."

"Your imagination starts to run wild."

Connie was contacted three hours after Faith's body was found, by a crisis counselor who told her little more than that her 19-year-old daughter Faith had been found dead in her apartment – the victim of what appeared to be a violent homicide.

"I said, 'you must have the wrong girl,'" Connie remembers. "She told me it was her, and I said, 'I don't think so.'"

It fell on Connie to contact the rest of the family, spreading the devastating news to her son, her ex-husband, and her eldest daughter, Rolanda. At that point, Connie said, she didn't have much to tell them other than that Faith was dead.

"They couldn't tell us very much because they didn't want to jeopardize the investigation," she explained. "Not knowing anything at all... your imagination starts to run wild."

Even after detectives brought the family to Chapel Hill, about 80 miles away from their home in Hollister, Connie still had no answers to her many questions. She wasn't even permitted to visit the crime scene, or see her youngest daughter.

"I just wanted to hold her hand, to let her know I was there," Connie recalled. "I still cry for my baby, and I wonder if she called out for help. Did she cry for me? These are the things you think."

Finally, the family was told the cause of death – but without any kind of motive or indication of what could have happened to lead up to Faith's murder, the new information was difficult for the family to process.

"It is getting harder, not knowing what happened, trying to accept what happened," said Rolanda. "She was beautiful. She didn't deserve it. She had a lot going for her."

While no arrests have been made, and no suspects even identified, Chapel Hill Police Lt. Josh Mecimore said police are still confident that the killer will be found and brought to justice.

"Someone knows something, and we're continually appealing to the public to come forward," he said. "This is not a cold case. We are still following up on things, still pounding the pavement, still waiting for that one piece of evidence that will help us solve this case."

Connie, Rolanda, and the rest of the Hedgepeth family are clinging to the same hope.

"At some point, God will let us know what happened," Rolanda said. "Even when I'm down, I still believe that we will find that person."

However, neighbours remain concerned as a result of the limited information available – and the fact that police have yet to make an arrest. While law enforcement officers continued to reassure nearby residents that the incident was an isolated event, neighbours wanted more answers.

"It's not a reassuring thought to wonder if you can send your kids to safety to the bus stop or if something could happen," said Anna Salomon, who lived with her husband and children in the subdivision next to the apartment complex where Faith was murdered. In the weeks following the killing, the neighbours banded together to walk children to the bus stop in collective groups.

Keeping Faith alive

One year after Faith was killed, students at the University of North Carolina gathered on campus at the Bell Tower Amphitheatre for a silent walk in celebration of the student's life. She was also made an honorary member of the Alpha Pi Omega Sorority, the country's oldest Native American Greek letter organization.

"She was the happiest person I knew, always laughing, always smiling," said Faith's friend Leslie Locklear.

Another friend, Victoria Chavis, remembered Faith's "bubbly personality."

"She had a smile that was just infectious," she said, "and she was a wonderful person to be around."

"The entire Carolina community grieves for the loss of this promising, vibrant student," added UNC Chancellor Carol Folt.

The family has honored Faith's memory by establishing the "Faith's Smile Scholarship" in her name – an award which will go to Native American women entering their freshman year of college. The scholarship project gives the family something positive to focus on while they continue searching for answers.

"It's really hard – hard because of not knowing what happened and not knowing why it happened, who did it," Rolanda added. "One little piece of information could break the case, could give us some type of peace. How could somebody withhold that, after everything we have lost?"

Still, for Connie, nothing can extinguish the shining light that defined her youngest daughter, Faith – no matter how many years go by with the case remaining unsolved.

"We don't want anyone to forget her smile. She was a beautiful girl, she was my baby," Connie said. "Her spirit is right here today."

THE MURDER OF IRA YARMOLENKO

On a seemingly normal Thursday afternoon on the Catawba River in May of 2008, two jet skiers planned on having a picnic together along the river when they stumbled upon a peculiar sight that would change their lives forever - a car crashed into a stump on the banks of the river along with the horrifying sight of a dead body lying next to it. They quickly alerted authorities and soon discovered that the body was that of a deceased young woman.

This was the tragic fate of Irina "Ira" Yarmolenko, a University of North Carolina college student who had just celebrated her twentieth birthday several days earlier. She was discovered with three items from her car tied around her neck. There was no sign of a struggle or any clear indication of a motive. She was not sexually assaulted or robbed.

Although first responders initially thought her death could have been a suicide, her death was ruled a homicide by asphyxiation. To this day, her murder still garners interest from the public due to the strange yet disturbing circumstances surrounding her death. Add to that the whispers that surround the case about the possibility that her convicted murderer, Mark Carver, might actually be an innocent man. What followed this horrific discovery was an investigation into the crime scene and into her personal life to uncover what happened to Ira.

Ira's early life and college experience

Ira Yarmolenko was born in the Ukraine on May 2nd, 1988 but emigrated to the United States when she was eight, along with her parents and brother Pavel. The family reportedly fled the Ukraine as refugees due to religious persecution. Her parents, both research scientists, were able to find job opportunities in North Carolina.

Ira quickly picked up the language and by all accounts seemed to assimilate well into American culture. She lived in North Carolina for most of her life, spoke with a southern accent and had several personal interests. Like most teenagers, she enjoyed hiking, acting, photography, sports, and music.

She also played the piano and liked listening to bands, such as the Counting Crows. She was also extremely academic. She excelled in math and science while being an active member of her high school poetry team. Ira was especially close to her family. Although she left Chapel Hill for UNC Charlotte, about a 3-hour drive away, she spoke to her mother almost every day. After her death, her mother said to reporters, "I don't think what I'm living is called life anymore."

During her two years in college, she found other interests beyond her required coursework at UNC Charlotte, where she was an undeclared major but had a strong interest in French. She was a photographer for the University Times, her college paper, and occasionally wrote columns and articles for the Niner Online, an online student-run newspaper.

She was also a member of the university's Russian Club as Russian was her first language. Her Russian language classmate described her as, "the kind of girl that always made you feel special, wanted, needed, cared for, and loved. It always seemed like she was always so happy to see you, and would always take at least a second of her time to say hello to you." It was here that she met her roommate Masha, another student from the Ukraine.

Masha and Ira bonded over the fact that they both spoke Russian and came from similar backgrounds. Masha described the day that she found out Ira was murdered when two investigators showed up at the small apartment that she shared with Ira, "It was her student I.D. picture. And I just started screaming. Sorry. Both of our families immigrated here to this country for a better life and sacrificed so much." Like most people close to Ira, Masha was devastated to hear the news of her friend's death.

Most people who knew Ira described her as outgoing. They felt that she would not have been afraid if a stranger had approached her. She was involved on campus and worked at a local coffee shop, Jackson's Java. Years after her death, her picture could still be found on the counter of Jackson's Java. She had a lasting impact on those that knew her. Her brother said, "Everything that she's ever done was to help people."

At UNC Charlotte, she had many close friends and acquaintances who described her as a cheerful and bubbly person, yet still high-achieving. In addition to her job at the coffee shop, Ira also worked as an aid in a computer lab on campus. The week before finals, her roommate Masha and friends threw a party for her 20th birthday.

During this party, her friends reported that Ira ended up cooking for everyone there, despite the fact that party was a celebration in her honor. This was not uncommon for her to do and was just the kind of person she was. Her friends concluded the celebration by visiting an art exhibit. They reported that she was in good spirits and that they parted amicably.

Although it seemed Ira was thriving in her environment at UNC Charlotte, she was in the process of closing her chapter there and beginning a new one at UNC-Chapel Hill, a school a bit closer to home. "Ira indicated she was sad to leave her friends behind at UNCC, but she was looking forward to attending UNC-Chapel Hill in the fall," according to Sgt. Tindall, an investigator in the case.

She had resigned from her positions at the coffee shop and in the computer lab where she had worked during her sophomore year shortly before she was murdered. Her brother Pavel, a then Ph.D. graduate student at Duke said, "She was not sure how she felt about leaving Charlotte. But she was very, very excited about coming to Chapel Hill."

Ira intended on transferring to UNC-Chapel Hill to be closer to her family and to major in public health. The day of her murder, she visited the coffee shop and said goodbye to her friends there and left a gift, a book, for her former boss. She also took several items to the Goodwill to donate and visited her credit union where she deposited some checks before heading to the river about 20 miles away.

The scene of the crime

The Catawba River is over 200 miles long and spans two states. It is located about 20 minutes from Charlotte and is popular among fisherman, boaters and jet skiers. First responders on that fateful day described a perplexing, yet disturbing scene.

The doors on the driver's side of Ira's car were opened, and her body was found just a few feet away. It did not appear she was sexually assaulted or robbed, nor did she have defensive wounds from fighting off her attacker or attackers.

Three ligatures were found around her neck: a nylon ribbon from a bag in her car, a drawstring from the hood of a jacket and a bungee cord. The drawstring was wrapped around her neck. The ribbon was wrapped once around her neck and oddly tied in a bow in the front. Her hair and body were also wet, although she was found on dry ground.

According to Detective Terry during the trial, "Her head was back towards the embankment. Her feet were near the river underneath some brush. Upon closer inspection, she was actually holding some of that brush in her hand. . . ." It was determined that this was the place where she was murdered and that she had not been transferred there.

Investigators began piecing together her movements before arriving at the river banks and determined it was likely that she headed down to the river banks to take pictures, as she was an avid photographer. Her brother Pavel said he "wasn't surprised she would go to such a remote spot. She was adventurous. She once hiked the Stampede Trail in Alaska with friends, searching for an abandoned bus made famous by Jon Krakauer's book Into the Wild."

Her camera was found in the trunk of her car, but there was not any film in it that could yield any clues about her death. Investigators quickly began interviewing people along the river to see if anyone had heard or seen anything out of the ordinary and came across two fishermen who were fishing about 100 yards from where Ira's body and car were discovered.

Mark Carver and Neil Cassada were cousins who grew up in the area and had been fishing in a new spot they had discovered the weekend before. This spot was about 100 yards from where Ira's car and body were discovered. Carver had been excited about the spot. He had returned to it because it did not require him to haul his boat to the river which was difficult for Carver to do since he suffers from carpal tunnel syndrome, a condition that makes his hands extremely weak.

His doctors recommended he not lift anything heavier than five pounds. Cassada also suffered from a heart condition, making it difficult to do anything too physical. Investigators questioned both men who reported that they had not seen Ira or had not heard anything from their fishing spot. They did report hearing a scraping sound that sounded like noise from construction.

They both willingly provided their DNA to investigators and went on their way. With the lack of forensic clues pointing toward any viable suspects, it was not until forensic analysis of the car several months later revealed partial DNA matches for Carver and Cassada that they became the prime suspects for Ira's murder. Mark Carver and Neal Cassada were arrested in December of 2008, seven months after her death and charged with conspiracy and murder. A day before Cassada's the trial began in 2010, Cassada died of a heart attack. Carver has always proclaimed their innocence.

"Simple" life of Mark Carver

Simple is the word often used to describe Mark Carver. "Simple in his routine, simple in his thought process, simple in his desires and wants," defense attorney Brent Ratchford said to reporters. Unlike Ira, Carver is not well-educated and has limitations with writing and reading comprehension, which he has struggled with throughout most of his life.

At an early age, he was placed in special education classes because of these limitations and his relatively low IQ. At 16, he dropped out of school to work in a mill. At the time he was arrested, it was documented that he was taking medication prescribed for schizophrenia.

Carver is also the father of four children from two different marriages. "He lived for his children and family," his sister-in-law Robin Carver said when asked about him. "He didn't really do much of anything else. Fishing and hunting and family, that was about it."

Although his family speaks well of Carver, like most family members often do, he did have prior brushes with the law despite never being convicted of a crime. In 2005, Carver faced a charge of injury to property. Carver purportedly confronted two people he thought were stealing his four-wheeler. The charge was dismissed, and the file no longer exists. A year before Ira's murder, Carver accidentally shot his son. Carver and his son were supposedly wrestling when the gun went off. "It was an accident," his son said. The case was later dismissed and Carver never convicted of a crime.

Cassada also had had his own dealings with the law. In 1995, he was accused of assault and injury to personal property. He reportedly pointed a gun at someone. But the charges were dismissed and the details remain unclear.

His family insists that he had nothing to do with Ira's murder and that the stress of the trial for a crime he did not commit ultimately led to his death. Kaye Cassada, Neal Cassada's wife said "After 37 years of loving that man and being married to that man, I know he is not capable of hurting anybody. He would have died to help somebody." Charges against Cassada were dropped, a common proceeding with deceased suspects. His family attended the hearing and his son Shannon Cassada said, "We want everybody to hear that he was an innocent man."

Carver also maintains his own innocence, stating "they said that they had ... my DNA and Neal's DNA in the car. I know that's a lie because Neal left, and they couldn't have gotten no DNA because I wasn't down there. I didn't go around it. I didn't go around the car. You know what

I'm saying?" He also said he didn't think Cassada would commit such a crime because "He's got four young'uns himself."

Although lie detector tests are not reliable enough to be used in court, during the initial investigation Cassada took a polygraph test, which he passed. Because he passed, investigators did not give Carver one. Carver has been very vocal about his willingness to also take a polygraph test.

Touch DNA

During the investigation and trial, Carver never wavered in proclaiming his innocence and said this to Ira's family "I never seen her that day. If I'd knowed she was up there, I would have went up there and helped her. They could have easily come down and killed me just like they did her."

His trial began in 2010. Before the trial, Carver was offered a surprising plea deal from the prosecution: 4-8 years in prison if he pleaded guilty to second degree murder. Had he taken this deal and pled guilty to murder he could be out of prison and with his family. His attorney said, "I have never gotten such a low offer. And to me that spoke volumes about the case." Carver turned down this offer and prosecutors moved forward with the case.

Prosecutors argued that the two men killed Ira because she witnessed or photographed something they did not want her to see. As a result, they strangled her and pushed her car on the embankment where their DNA was transferred to the car. Their intention was to sink the car in the water, but it hit a stump where it stayed until it was finally discovered by the jet skiers. They then returned to their fishing spot until they were questioned by police.

Prosecutors relied on a relatively new forensic technique at the time known as "touch DNA." Unlike previous methods, touch DNA uses smaller amounts of DNA, such as skin cells transferred to a person or object when they come into contact with someone. But touch DNA is not as reliable as other DNA methods requiring blood or saliva because it is difficult to determine the origin of these cells. For instance, skin cells can be transferred indirectly by a third party or carrier.

For example, a man in California was falsely imprisoned because his DNA was found on a murder victim. It was determined that it was impossible that he was a killer because he had a solid alibi. At the time of the murder, he was unconscious in a hospital due to extreme intoxication.

Prosecutors then discovered that the same paramedic who treated him for intoxication was a first responder at the murder scene. The DNA from the intoxicated man was presumably transferred to the victim by the paramedic. This case set a precedent about the reliability of touch DNA and is cited by Carver's advocates for innocence as a possibility as to why Carver's and Cassada's DNA was found on Ira's car.

Despite this interesting theory, it was not presented by the defense in Carver's trial and the jury found him guilty of murder. He was sentenced to and is currently serving life in prison. Carver's advocates argue that the car and crime scene was not preserved, and that Carver and Cassada's DNA could have been transferred by officers or other people near the crime scene. Many officers, the jet skiers, first responders were all present at the crime scene and could have all inadvertently transferred the DNA to the car.

Several other inconsistencies exist in the prosecution's case. Carvers DNA was not found on her body nor on the trunk of the car where he and Cassada would have pushed it into the river bank according to prosecutors. Carvers DNA did not match a third DNA profile found on the bungee cord and the only DNA found under Ira's fingernails was her own.

His attorney and advocates also argue that the two men couldn't have physically pushed the car into the river bank due to Carver's carpal tunnel and Cassada's heart condition. Cassada supposedly got winded just walking. In 2013, Carver's attorneys filed an appeal on his behalf, but the appeals court determined "no error in the defendant's trial" occurred, meaning his conviction of life in prison would be upheld. But this did not deter his advocates from trying to prove Carver did not receive a fair defense during his trial.

Earlier this year, a judge granted the request of the North Carolina Actual Innocence Project, attorneys who have become interested in Carver case who believe Carver is wrongfully imprisoned, to see DNA reports that were never shared with Carvers defense team, along with further DNA testing.

They argue that Carver did not receive a proper defense as his lawyers did not call any witnesses or DNA experts to the stand and address the DNA evidence, and that the DNA evidence is not compelling enough beyond a reasonable doubt to warrant a life sentence for Carver. It is the only evidence linking Carver to the crime. Only time will determine the final outcomes of Carver's appeals as the evidentiary hearing has been postponed. Legal proceedings could take several years.

Other suspects

If Carver and Cassada's DNA was indeed transferred by a third party and they did not kill Ira, then who did? There was no one in her life that seemed to have any motive. Besides these two men, there was only one other suspect in her murder investigation. Nine months after the murder, Christopher Lemont Cooper wrote a letter to News anchor Erica Bryant to "confess a sin," that he and several other accomplices had killed Ira.

He said he drove a van full of friends that were all high and needed money for drugs. He said he was unable to sleep "because of what we did to that young woman." And wished to meet with the reporter. The TV station did not publish the letter and turned it over to investigators where they took the letter very seriously and launched an investigation with the North Carolina State Bureau of Investigations.

Police and investigators visited Cooper, where he was in jail on charges of rape, assault by strangulation, and for being delinquent in child support. He reportedly refused to cooperate with investigators, but they ultimately ruled him out as a suspect concluding that several of the accomplices he named were incarcerated at the time of the murder. They also cleared the other accomplices named in Cooper's letter and continued building their case against Carver and Cassada.

Free Mark Carver

Free Mark Carver is one of the prominent websites advocating for the release of Carver. They believe he is innocent or at the very least did not receive a proper defense in his trial. The website is run by a former newspaper journalist who now works in the fashion industry. She had no ties to the case or families and became intrigued with the case in 2011 after its details aired on Dateline NBC and through other online news articles.

One of the major theories from Carver's advocates presented on the website is that Ira was not murdered and in fact committed suicide by placing the ligatures around her neck herself. They claim that Ira was not the cheerful person described by her friends and loved ones and that she had battled depression.

Her boyfriend had broken up with her shortly before her murder and her poetry was sometimes dark and melancholy. The website alludes to accounts from unnamed people who claim that Ira had attempted suicide when she was younger and had seen a therapist at UNC Charlotte. The website does not provide sources and only mentions them as letters to the author.

Although this theory may be offensive to those who loved Ira and describe her as a happy and vibrant young woman, it has been addressed by pathologists who have dismissed this theory saying "For this to have been anything but a homicide, i.e., this was a suicide, this victim would have to tie three ligatures around her neck tightly and before death get into this position while that's going on and her legs underneath the brush given that position and I just feel like that was not consistent with what we are seeing. . . . Yes, and another thing that this illustrates a little bit better also is the presence of particular matter, soil and grass on her skirt as well. So that's another thing that would have had to happen. If this was a suicide she would have had to do all this stuff by herself. It is just not consistent with that theory."

Her brother Pavel, who has since completed his Ph.D. in biomedical engineering and continues to conduct research at a pediatric hospital, said he has read some of the internet theories about his sister's death, but they are "not grounded in reality." He asserts that his sister never attempted suicide and there was no indication she was depressed. Nevertheless, the fact remains that a lively, young woman lost her life just days after her 20th birthday.

Memorials

We may never know what really happened to Ira or why someone chose to take her life but it is clear that she touched many people who strive to keep her memory alive. The jet skiers who found her body, Dennis Lovelace and Brenda Pierce, placed a memorial cross where they found her car. The changing levels of the Catawba river sometimes covers part of the cross, but it is still visible to visitors.

A memorial bench as far as Alaska, where Ira spent a summer waitressing, also bears her name. "A Kansas City based artist Shane Blindt designed and installed this bench at the request of many co-workers whose lives were touched with Ira's presence during the 2007 McKinley Village

Lodge summer season. Lettering on the memorial was hand drawn with pen showing the elegance and beauty of Ira's outward expressions contrasted with a raw and rugged placement into the world she left behind." It is maintained by locals there.

Her high school poetry team in Chapel Hill renamed the group The Sacrificial Poets in her honor.

What Time Devours is a book written by her former professor at UNC Charlotte who dedicated his book to her memory. He directed a campus production, which Ira was a part of the previous year before she was murdered. He also included a line from her poetry and her picture in the dedication of the book.

The controversy around her murder continues to intrigue people and several websites and pages are dedicated to outlining the details of the case. Ira's murder has been featured on Dateline and 20/20. She continues to captivate an almost cult following, and many people are still tirelessly working to prove that Carver is innocent and did not receive a fair trial. If this is the case, it means that justice has not been served for Ira and her family. But one thing is for sure, the memory of Ira Yarmolenko will continue to live on with her family, friends, and strangers that have been touched by her story.

THE DISAPPEARANCE OF KELSIE SCHELLING

52

ANA BENSON

Every time a woman goes missing or is found murdered, the police usually takes a closer look at their spouses or boyfriends. It is a standard procedure, especially if there were indications that they were in a troubled relationship. The disappearance of Kelsie Schelling is one of the biggest mysteries in Colorado. This young pregnant woman was last seen in February of 2013 and the case is still open to this day.

However, Kelsie's family was quite disappointed at the lack of interest by the police to investigate her then-boyfriend Donthe Lucas, who was clearly involved in this crime. After all, Donthe did invite Kelsie to his hometown on that fateful night and he was the last person who saw her alive. When they realized that the police are stalling with the investigation, the family made a promise that Kelsie's case will not be forgotten until they discover what really happened. They kept the public informed through their Facebook page and eventually managed to reach the Colorado Bureau of Investigation.

Early life

Kelsie Jean Schelling was born on 18th February 1991 in Holyoke, Colorado. She grew up in a tightknit family and later became even closer to her mother after the divorce of her parents. Kelsie was only eleven years old when they split up but she would often talk to her father as well. However, they didn't see each other that often because he moved to a different part of town. After graduating from high school, Kelsie attended Northeastern Junior College located in Sterling, Colorado. She was fascinated with psychology and planned to major in it once she gets accepted to the university.

Kelsie was friendly and outspoken, so it comes as no surprise that she had many friends and was a life of every party. During her time at Northeastern Junior College, Kelsie met Donthe Lucas. He was a star player on the basketball team and the two of them fell in love instantly. Donthe Lucas had a very difficult childhood and he grew up in Pueblo, Colorado which is an infamous place known for higher crime rates than anywhere else in the state. He loved basketball and it was clear that he would be an outstanding athlete even in high school. Basketball players do have enormous salaries so Donthe Lucas did see it as an opportunity to help his family out further down the line.

He was hoping that a scout would attend one of his games and recruit him for one of bigger colleges or universities that had a good basketball team. But his big break never happened. Instead, he ended up in Northeastern Junior College which was alright, but Donthe wasn't quite happy with that outcome. His dissatisfaction was evident even in the relationship with Kelsie. Their romance had constant ups and downs, and the two of them would break up, and get back together which drove Kelsie mad. They did finally call it quits after several semesters, and didn't see each other for quite some time.

After finishing the two years at the junior college, Kelsie pursued her education even further, and she moved to California to attend Vanguard University in Costa Mesa. She was finally able to study psychology full time. Donthe continued to play basketball for Emporia State University in Kansas. Kelsie's family was happy she managed to end her relationship with the troubled basketball player, and they hoped that she would make a new life far away from Colorado. Kelsie was independent and she enjoyed living and studying in California. When she wasn't attending classes, Kelsie worked at a tanning salon with her best friend. However, she did drop out of the college because the school work was a bit too much for her at the time and her only option was to go back home. She moved to Denver in 2012 and started working in a store. Meanwhile, Donthe Lucas was back in his hometown Pueblo.

The two of them started talking once again during the autumn of 2012. It was obvious that they still had feelings for each other, so no one was surprised when Donthe and Kelsie decided to spend the Christmas holidays together. The couple seemed happy to everyone around them, but Kelsie did tell her friends that their relationship was still very toxic. Donthe was still treating her badly, calling her names, and starting unnecessary fights. Soon enough everything will change. A few weeks after the holidays, Kelsie found out that she was pregnant. Shocked at first, Kelsie was lost and decided not to tell anyone for a couple of weeks. But keeping a secret was hard. So she called her mother and told her the news. Kelsie's mother Laura would later say that even though her daughter felt a bit stressed, she was still excited about the pregnancy. Yes, she was young but Kelsie was determined to make it work.

Donthe Lucas didn't take the news so well. Having in mind how dissatisfied he felt about his failed basketball career, it is not wrong to assume that the news about a baby simply solidified the fact that his dreams will never come true. Kelsie noticed the change in his mood and openly told him that he doesn't have to be a part of their baby's life. But it is also worth mentioning that Kelsie confided in her best friend that Donthe was ecstatic to become a father at one point. However, his mind was constantly changing. Kelsie went to see her doctor on 4th of February 2013 and he confirmed that she was eight weeks pregnant. The baby was healthy and doing well. The doctor provided her with an ultrasound of the unborn baby, and she was full of joy. Kelsie immediately sent out the pictures to her mother, her friends, and Donthe. Unfortunately, the excitement will not last forever.

The night of the disappearance

Donthe and Kelsey exchanged several emails on February 3rd, 2013. He invited her to visit him in Pueblo. She turned him down saying that she needs to go for a checkup the next day to make sure everything is alright with the baby. After seeing her doctor on the morning of February 4th, 2013, Kelsie went straight to the store. She worked the second shift and was expected to come home sometime after 10:00 PM that night. However, she was in contact with Donthe for the entire day, texting back and forth about the pregnancy. Donthe told her that she should drive out to Pueblo after work because he had a surprise for her. Not knowing what it is, Kelsie asked for more information because Pueblo is two hours away from Denver, and she would probably be tired after work. He insisted that she would be happy with his surprise and that he cannot tell her anything over the phone.

It is safe to assume that Kelsie thought that Donthe was ready to change and start a family with her. Their relationship wasn't a standard one but it seemed like Kelsie was willing to move past all the negative things and focus on the future. So after her shift ended, Kelsie got in her Chevy Cruze LTZ and drove to Pueblo in the middle of the night. Donthe was supposed to meet her in a parking lot in front of a local Walmart. The surveillance cameras did confirm that Kelsie got there on time, but Donthe was nowhere to be seen. She waited in a parked car for almost an hour before sending another text message to Donthe, saying that she has been in the parking lot for too long and that she would come pick him up at whatever location he is at the moment. She got a reply sometime around 12:15 AM.

Donthe told her that he will be waiting for her in the street next to his grandmother's home. Kelsie is seen exiting the parking lot a couple of minutes after she got the message. She clearly did arrive at the second rendezvous spot, but once again Donthe wasn't there. Kelsie sent him another message asking where is he and Donthe replied that he will be there in a minute. This is the last known communication between these two until sometime before 04:00 AM. After going through the phone records, police did discover that Donthe called Kelsie at 03:54 AM but she didn't pick up. The significance of this mysterious phone call will be revealed later. After reviewing the cell tower pings for both phones, the investigators did discover that they were in close proximity to each other.

The search for Kelsie

Kelsie's mother Laura got really worried the next day because she wasn't able to reach her daughter over the phone. She tried calling numerous times but it went straight to the voicemail. The last message she got from her daughter was the ultrasound image of her unborn child, and Laura wasn't sure if something happened to Kelsie after work, or she was ignoring her calls. Laura contacted Kelsie's friends who told her that she went to Pueblo to meet with Donthe. With no word from her daughter, she called Donthe who picked up his phone and told Laura that he had seen Kelsie last night, but that she drove back home in the morning.

Laura was starting to panic, but she did tell Donthe that she would involve the police if she doesn't hear from her daughter soon. Laura and Kelsie were very close and they did tell each other everything, but she suspected that her daughter kept this information from her because she didn't want Laura to know that she was meeting with Donthe. After all, Laura was aware of the nature of their relationship, and his reluctance to accept the baby. Plus, Laura would probably advise Kelsie not to go to Pueblo in the middle of the night.

Laura contacted the local law enforcement and told them that her daughter was missing. Without any solid leads or evidence, they started asking around for Kelsie. Their first step was to take a closer look at Donthe because he claimed that he was the last person to saw Kelsie. She did travel from Denver just to see him. After checking Kelsie's credit card records, they did notice that the card was used hours after Kelsie's last known contact with Donthe. They reviewed the surveillance of the ATM and noticed that Donthe had the card and picked up $400 from Kelsie's account. They weren't sure if Donthe had Kelsie's agreement to use the card, but that was a felony in the state of Colorado, so he was led to the police station for questioning. He had a lot of things to clear up, starting with the timeline of Kelsie's visit to Pueblo.

Donthe's interview

After being picked up by the police, Donthe told his own version of the story. They did see each other that night and talked until early morning hours. Donthe and Kelsie got into a fight and she felt too agitated to drive back home to Denver. She was also very tired from working the second shift. Instead, Kelsie decided to sleep in her car which was parked near his grandmother's house. According to Donthe, his phone rang sometime around 07:00 AM and it was Kelsie. She wasn't feeling well and asked Donthe to drive her to a hospital. He put on his clothes, got to her car, and drove her to the Parkview Hospital.

Kelsie wasn't sure if something happened to the baby during their argument last night and she insisted to see a doctor before she heads out to Denver. Donthe sat inside her car in the parking lot for two hours when she finally emerged from the hospital. Kelsie told him that she had lost the baby. She then asked Donthe to drive her to Walmart to get something to eat and buy some snacks for the road. The two of them started fighting while they were in Walmart and Kelsie refused to drive him home. Donthe simply walked away and got to his grandmother's house on foot. He didn't see Kelsie later in the day and he assumed she went home. He didn't mention stopping at the ATM to pick up the money during his initial interview.

The investigators did notice a couple of possible leads that could collaborate Donthe's story, namely the Parkview Hospital. Each medical facility keeps detailed records of the patients they treat. After speaking to the staff and going through the data, they have confirmed that Kelsie didn't check in during the morning of February 5th. There were also numerous surveillance cameras all over the building and none of them picked up Kelsie entering or leaving the hospital. It was obvious that this part of Donthe's story was not true.

Of course, the police investigators decided to check out Walmart as well because the parking lot and stores do have surveillance cameras, and they might have picked up something that would be of use. While they couldn't find Kelsie or Donthe entering the Walmart, they did notice Kelsie's car on the parking lot. However, the timeline didn't match up with Donthe's story because Kelsie's car appeared at noon, and not in the morning. Plus, Donthe was the only passenger in the car. Another surveillance camera which was positioned on the back side of Walmart did record Donthe getting into his mother's car – another detail he failed to mention in the initial talk with the investigators.

Without any proof that Donthe's version of the events is true, they called him up for a second interview. The investigators did have a plan this time - they wanted to find out more about the ATM, and how it fits into his timeline. He told the detectives that he took $400 in order to pay his bills and that Kelsie lent him the money since he was at the ATM while Kelsie was at the hospital. When the detectives told Donthe that there is no record of Kelsie ever being in that hospital, his reply was: "I don't even know what to say right now."

They also presented him with Walmart surveillance video that proves Donthe was the only person in the car. He was surprised with the evidence put in front of him, and before the detectives managed to get him to open up, he decided to lawyer up. He was only charged with the identity theft due to the fact that he used Kelsie's credit card, but the case was dropped. The judge had determined that Donthe did use Kelsie's credit card in the past and it was a normal behavior. However, nobody managed to figure out why Donthe had her card in the first place. After all, if Kelsie decided to ran away and start a new life, she would need the money, as well as her vehicle.

Speaking of Kelsie's car, the investigators took a closer look at the surveillance video from Walmart parking lot because they wanted to follow the vehicle. Exactly one day after Donthe left Kelsie's car there, another man approached the car and got inside by using the key. He didn't break in or steal the car. The man was dressed in black, wearing a hoodie, so identifying him was almost impossible. His body type was different than Donthe's, and the mystery man was significantly shorter. Keep in mind that Donthe was a tall basketball player, so his height would be noticeable, even in a low-quality video.

Seeing the direction in which the car went, the police collected the surveillance videos from stores and businesses which were in close proximity. They put the puzzle pieces together and found a route but they couldn't follow it all the way. One day later, the car was dropped at the parking lot of Saint Mary Corwin Hospital. The man locked the car and walked away. The investigators located the vehicle on 14th of February, 2013 and figured out the timeline. But nobody knows where the car was during 6th of February. There weren't any signs of a struggle that would indicate that Kelsie was killed in her car. Almost all of her personal items were missing, including her wallet and a backpack.

While it is unclear if the vehicle was tested for the traces of DNA, an unnamed police officer who worked for Pueblo Police Department will later say that they did find bodily fluids in the trunk of Kelsie's car, as well as two palm prints. However, no one knows what happened with this evidence and was it ever tested. It is simply another thing which the police investigators decided to ignore in this case. Unfortunately, the whole investigation will be under scrutiny soon after.

Theories

Figuring out a solid theory without too many evidence or information can be challenging. Laura, Kelsie's mother, claims that her daughter was probably murdered and that it was premeditated. The first red flag for her was Donthe's initial invitation to meet him before the doctor's appointment. When Kelsie refused, he knew that he had to act fast. Donthe lured Kelsie to Pueblo by saying that he has something to show her, but he never gave an explanation to the law enforcement about what the surprise really was.

It is clear that Kelsie was alive and well up until the point she met Donthe in the street next to his grandmother's house. This is where the trail goes cold. The activity on her phone stops until 04:00 AM. If we analyze the location of the phones, another theory is that Donthe led Kelsie to a remote location and harmed her. It was possible that Kelsie dropped her phone in the middle of a struggle. Donthe couldn't find the phone in the dark, so he had to call her number. He was very likely getting rid of the evidence.

There is a possibility that the two of them did indeed get into a fight, and that an unfortunate accident happened. However, it is more likely that Donthe planned to get rid of Kelsie, and had planned every single step he would take that night. He really insisted to see her as soon as possible. While it is not fair to put the blame on the rest of Lucas family, the fact that his mother picked him up immediately after he left Kelsie's vehicle at the Walmart's parking lot indicates that she knew what was going on. Pueblo Police Department did stop investigating Donthe, and they claimed they didn't have enough physical evidence to prove that a crime really occurred. But they did receive a couple of noteworthy tips which were ignored and never pursued.

The missed opportunities

The entire investigation of the disappearance of Kelsie Schelling was troubling from the very beginning. While the detectives did not have physical evidence of a crime, it was clear that Donthe was the last person who saw Kelsie alive. In every standard investigation, he would have been the prime suspect, and the investigators would do their best to find more proof that he was somehow connected to the crime. The cell tower pings did show that both of their phones were in a remote area next to Pueblo in the early morning hours.

But there are even bigger missed opportunities that could have provided the investigators with the proof they needed. For instance, Donthe was living in his grandmother's house at the time of Kelsie's disappearance. However, the entire family moved out soon after. The landlord started redecorating the house because he wanted to rent it again. He did hear about the missing girl from Denver but had no idea about the details of the case, or the fact that the Lucas family was involved in any way.

He decided to put the new carpets in and when he lifted the old one, the landlord noticed a strange stain on the bottom. He contacted the police enforcement because he was worried that something bad has happened in the house. However, the police ignored his request to check out the stained carpet, and no one had ever arrived at Lucas' previous residence to pick it up. The landlord ended up throwing the carpet away because he simply couldn't keep it forever in the house and wanted to move on with the renovation.

Another missed opportunity involved a couple of fishermen who were out on a lake on a night fishing expedition. It is important to mention that the lake was located near the Saint Mary Corwin Hospital. As you might recall, that was the spot where the police officers discovered Kelsie's vehicle on the 14th of February 2013. They were out on a bank when a hook got stuck to something poking out of the sand. The fishermen went to investigate and were sure that they saw a part of a human ribcage, as well as a skull.

They were terrified by that discovery and left the area right away. Both of them were reluctant to notify the police because they did have some troubles with the law in the past. But that didn't stop them from telling this story to their friends who urged them to contact the local law enforcement. A couple of months passed before they finally talked to the police, but the lake wasn't searched afterward.

The current searches

Family and friends continued to search for Kelsie even after it was clear that the police enforcement forgot about her case. They created a Facebook group that was constantly updated with new information. Pueblo Police Department did go through many changes after Kelsie went missing. The lead investigator was replaced with a new one who was willing to cooperate with the Schelling family. The Schellings did offer a large reward for any new leads that might help them locate their missing daughter. The reward was $100,000 at one point.

This eventually led to false claims and misleading messages such as the one which claimed that Kelsie was still alive, but was placed into a sex traffic ring after a hired hitman decided not to kill her. Laura Schelling contacted the police and told them about the message. Since the investigators decided to follow every lead possible, they dug deeper and even involved the FBI. Their experts did manage to trace the message back to Russia through the IP address so it was clear that this tip was useless.

The biggest break in the case happened in the spring of 2017 when Colorado Bureau of Investigation finally got the authorization from the local law enforcement to join the search. CBI did determine that the prime suspect should be Donthe Lucas, and they got the warrant to search the area around his previous place of residence. A large number of police officers was seen around that house during April of 2017, and they dug up the parts of the backyard using heavy machinery.

The search has been successful and the officers left the scene carrying bags of evidence. However, they stated that they didn't find any traces of Kelsie's remains. Kelsie's family released the following statement after the search: "The past 2 days have been grueling and emotional, ending with the outcome we did not hope for. Kelsie is still missing. There is no way for me to convey to you all the pain that I feel right now. Sincere, heartfelt thanks goes out to the members of Pueblo PD, CBI and Parks & Rec who worked so hard on this search for Kelsie. This was a physically demanding excavation for them and we witnessed how hard they worked. Despite all the issues we have had in the past, the new leadership over Kelsie's case from PPD and active involvement from CBI is giving us hope that an effective investigation is finally taking place."

The case is still active and the police didn't arrest Donthe. But the positive changes are happening and Kelsie's family is certain that they will find the answers they are looking for now that the investigation is finally moving forward.

THE MURDER OF KARYN KUPCINET

OLIVIA WATSON

Chapter 1

In the latter half of 1963, Karyn Kupcinet was living in Hollywood while pursuing her one true dream: to become a famous starlet. She was constantly on the lookout for the role that would land her her big break. From an outsider's perspective, Kupcinet was well-equipped for and well on her way to stardom. Her life had all the ingredients: she had a wealthy, well-known father, an actor boyfriend whose career was gaining steam, and dark sultry looks that many would have died for. However, behind the scenes, not all was as it seemed.

In reality, Kupcinet's life was on a dramatic downward spiral in the latter half of 1963. Her relationship with her boyfriend, Andrew Prine, was strained at best and her mental health was deteriorating since undergoing an illegal abortion in July of that year. On November 28, 1963, she was dead.

Karyn Kupcinet's life began in a much-less dramatic manner than in which it was taken though. Karyn Kupcinet was born on March 6, 1941 in Chicago. As a young child, she acquired the nickname "Cookie." That was what her parents liked to call her, so was so sweet she'd give you a toothache.

Karyn did not get her sweet side from her mother though. Esther Kupcinet was often described as not caring about anyone unless they were famous. It was no surprise when she began grooming her young daughter to become an actress. She was from the Gold Coast in Chicago, a picturesque neighborhood that's home to Chicago's most affluent residents. Esther herself was a failed wannabe-dancer who imparted a love of the fame-filled lifestyle into her young daughter.

Her mother, Esther Kupcinet, would be the one to encourage Karyn to pursue acting as a career later in her life, but it would be her father who gave her the means to do so. Karyn's father was Irv Kupcinet, was a well-known and well-respected newspaper columnist for the *Chicago Sun-Times* who also worked as a television talk-show host and radio personality. To many in Chicago, he was known simply, but immediately, as "Kup."

Earlier in his life, Kupcinet was a Philadelphia Eagle. Kupcinet joined the NFL team after playing for the University of North Dakota. He was signed in 1935, and many thought he had a long career ahead of him playing for the team. Unfortunately, after playing only part of his first season, Kupcinet sustained a serious shoulder injury which benched him for the remainder of the season. After surgery Kupcinet was told that his shoulder would never fully recover, so Irv retired from his short run in the NFL.

After retiring from the NFL, Irv Kupcinet decided to combine his love and knowledge of sports with another passion of his that he developed in high school—reporting. Kupcinet took a job as a sports writer for the *Chicago Daily Times*. Kupcinet flourished at the job, and soon began writing about more than just sports. In 1948, Kupcinet was given his own column, *Kup's Column*, which chronicled the nightlife and celebrity scene of Chicago.

Kupcinet's success with the *Chicago Daily Times* filtered through many aspects of his career. The paper had built up his fame, and Kupcinet was now well-known in Chicago. In 1952, Kupcinet translated his fame for television when he landed his own talk show. Later, he was part of a group of talented talk show hosts who replaced Steve Allen on *The Tonight Show*.

By the time Kupcinet launched his talk show in 1952, he was almost a household name in Chicago. Thirty-four years and 15 Emmy Awards later, Kupcinet was a household name across America.

In 1957, Irv's daughter, Karyn Kupcinet, was in high school. She was 16 years old and starting to think about her future for the first time. She knew she wanted to be in the spotlight, she was a natural beauty and she admired her father's fame. Her mother suggested she pursue acting and Karyn loved the idea. She had participated in school plays since she was thirteen but had never thought of pursuing acting as a career before. Karyn soon discovered that having a father with his own television show syndicated on over 70 stations across America opened a lot of doors in Hollywood.

Chapter 2

During high school, Karyn Kupcinet decided she wanted to become a famous actress. She spent her senior year applying to arts colleges across the country and was accepted to Pine Manor College. After graduation, Kupcinet left her hometown and family for Boston, determined to hone her acting skills at the liberal arts college.

Kupcinet's time at Pine Manor was short-lived though. In fact, the young starlet-to-be studied in Boston for only a single semester before packing back up and moving to New York City. In New York, Kupcinet began studying at the Actors Studio, a membership organization for those who are determined to succeed in the world of show business.

Through connections she made at the Actors Studio, and through connections with producers she acquired through her father, Karyn landed her first professional role in the 1961 Jerry Lewis film *The Ladies Man*. In her first role, Kupcinet played a bit part as a young lady in a Hollywood boardinghouse alongside dozens of other young starlet wannabes.

Amongst the crowd of young ladies, Kupcinet managed to stand out. The same year, she appeared in two episodes of *Hawaiian Eye*, an episode of *The Andy Griffith Show*, and an episode of *The Donna Reed Show*.

Kupcinet was getting positive reviews for her roles, and went on to guest star in many other popular television shows. In 1962 she was awarded roles in *The Red Skeleton Show*, and *G.E. True*.

As well as these guest roles, Kupcinet also landed her first starring role in 1962 on the primetime series *Mrs. G. Goes to College*, which was later retitled *The Gertrude Berg Show* for its run. The premise of *The Gertrude Berg Show* was that a middle-aged Jewish widow enrolls in a college as a freshman after her children are all grown up. While at college, she interacts with a variety of younger students and her Cambridge University exchange professor, who was played by Cedric Hardwicke.

Kupcinet played the role of Carol, a classmate of Mrs. G. who dated her good friend Joe Caldwell, who was played by Skip Ward. Kupcinet's character had little dialogue, but her dark, sultry looks stood out from the background.

In 1962, Kupcinet also completed one of her first interviews as an actress on the rise. She was interviewed by the *Los Angeles Times* to help promote *Mrs. G. Goes to College*. This interview was supposed to promote her profile as a hirable, talented actress as well, but many instead thought it provided insight into the extreme pressure the young starlet was facing.

During the interview, Kupcinet spoke highly of her cast mates and the show, but had a difficult time talking about her own involvement in the program. When the questions turned to herself, Kupcinet talked exclusively about food and her body weight.

Despite facing an inner pressure, Kupcinet won more acting roles, which she was praised for. After *Mrs. G. Goes to College* finished its short run, Kupcinet appeared in *The Wide Country,* and *Going My Way*. While her role in these shows were short, her work on *The Wide Country* garnered the attention of one person in particular—the show's star Andrew Prine.

Andrew Prine was an actor who came to Hollywood from Florida in 1957 when he first appeared in a single episode of *U.S. Steel Hour*. By 1962, Prine had hit it big. In the same year, Prine was cast in both the Academy Award-nominated film, *The Miracle Worker*, as Helen Keller's older brother, and in the lead role of the NBC series *The Wide Country*.

The Wide Country was an American Western drama about two brothers who worked in the travelling rodeo circuit. The older brother Mitch, played by Earl Holliman, warns his brother about the dangers of following in his own footsteps in the bronco riding world, but Prine's character, Andy, refuses to listen.

In December of 1962, Andrew Prine crossed Karyn Kupcinet's path when she guest starred on *The Wide Country*. On screen, their characters never interacted, but off screen, the pair couldn't keep their eyes, or their hands, off one another.

The two rising stars began dating each other, and on paper they seemed to be a match made in heaven. They were both young, attractive, and chasing stardom. In reality, however, the relationship was very strained.

Once the puppy love phase of their relationship passed, Prine was hesitant to make the relationship exclusive. They were both busy workers with packed schedules and they were young. Prine had just begun to make his mark in Hollywood, and didn't want to settle down or dedicate too much of his time to another person. Most of all, though, Prine was worried that Kupcinet would be a mar on his good reputation.

Although she was receiving good review for her work, Kupcinet was beginning to crumble under the enormous pressure she felt to follow in her father's footsteps of success. Kupcinet began abusing diet pills in 1961. Diet pills in the 1960s were not the same as they are today. Little was known about the properties of many ingredients, so the FDA often approved substances that were not safe for consumption.

One of the most popular diet pills at the time was Obetrol, which was approved by the FDA on January 19, 1960. Obetrol was marketed as a way to lose and control a person's weight. It was a popular drug at the time, and many believed that it was effective in helping them feel more energetic and lose weight quicker, which is not surprising as it was a formulation of three amphetamine mixed salts, including methamphetamine.

Along with her addiction to diet pills, Kupcinet also began abusing prescription drugs in the early 1960s. This combination proved too much for Kupcinet, who began to deteriorate. Despite coming from a wealthy family who were happy to support the young star, Kupcinet began shoplifting from popular stores and was arrested in 1963 for stealing two books, a sweater, and a pair of capris pants. Andrew Prine was mortified by Kupcinet's arrest, worried about how it would reflect on him through their connection.

By August of 1963, Karyn Kupcinet's relationship with Andrew Prine was all but over. In the previous month, Kupcinet underwent an illegal abortion in Tijuana after becoming pregnant with Prine's child. Prine had encouraged Kupcinet to undergo the procedure to protect both of their reputations and because he had no intention of marrying Kupcinet as she had hoped.

After the procedure, Prine declared their relationship over and began dating other women, but Kupcinet wasn't about to let her first love end quite yet.

Chapter 3

By the latter half of 1963, Karyn Kupcinet had lost her touch on reality. Her first love, Andrew Prine, had finally severed all ties to the young starlet due to her addiction to prescription and diet pills, but she wasn't ready to let go. Kupcinet began stalking Prine at his home, and would write about these experiences in her diary.

July 30th read, *Andy with Anna. Me watched from hedge. Awful. Nightmares.*

August 20th followed, *So humiliated by Andy's lack of interest.*

On October 29th she wrote, *Andy acting ugly. Complete indifference. Scene at his house. I'm hysterical.*

While these short messages tell a foreboding tale, the worst entries came from November.

On the 4th, after hiding in Prine's attic, she wrote *Wish I were dead*, and 24 days later on November 28, 1963, she was.

Months before her death, though, Kupcinet put a great deal of effort into making her Prine believe that her life, and his, were in great danger.

Along with stalking Prine and his new girlfriends at his house, Kupcinet began sending letters to Prine. But these were no ordinary letters. Kupcinet would put together threatening and profanity-filled hate mail composed of words cut from magazines. She sent these letters anonymously to Prine, sometimes skipping the post and dropping them off right on his doorstep.

But Prine suspected Kupcinet was behind these letters, so he confronted her. Luckily for her, Kupcinet had thought ahead and composed several similar letters to herself, claiming they had also been anonymously sent to her. She was hoping this would inspire a desire to protect in Prine, but he remained wary of his unstable ex.

Prine always remembered these startling letters. After Kupcinet's death, he had police examine the letters to see if they could determine who had sent them. The answer was no surprise to him. Investigators were able to find Kupcinet's fingerprints all over them, including on the sticky side of the scotch tape used to secure the frightening messages to the paper.

On the night of November 28, 1963, Kupcinet had dinner with her close friends Mark Goddard and his wife Marcia Rogers Goddard at their Beverly Hills House. She was an hour late for dinner, arriving at 7:30p.m. when the dinner had begun at 6:30p.m. The Goddard's later told police that Kupcinet was surprised they had waited for her to eat, and she hardly touched her food throughout the meal.

This was normal for Kupcinet though, who had struggled with body issues and the pressure to stay thin since high school. What wasn't normal, however, was the state Kupcinet was in. Marcia Goddard told authorities that that night Kupcinet acted very strangely during their last meal together. Her lips seemed numb and her voice sounded funny. She moved her head at odd angles and her pupils were incredibly small.

Mark Goddard had confronted Kupcinet about this odd behaviour during the meal, accusing her of being high. Kupcinet immediately began to cry and deny being on any substances and instead blamed her behaviour on the unsubstantiated claim that she had found an abandoned baby on her doorstep earlier that day.

An hour after she arrived, Kupcinet left the Goddard's house in a taxi cab headed home. She promised to call her friends the next day when she was feeling better. After arriving home, she was visited by two friends of hers, Edward Rubin and Robert Hathaway, who also happened to be neighbors and close friends with her ex-boyfriend.

According to Hathaway and Rubin, the three friends watched TV and had coffee with Kupcinet before she fell asleep beside them on the couch. They woke her up and helped her get to her bedroom. After this, the men said they turned the TV off, locked the doors, and left around 11:15p.m.

The men then headed over to Robert Hathaway's house where they were joined by Andrew Prine himself. The three friends chatted and watched TV until 3:00a.m.

The next day, the Goddard's waited for Karyn Kupcinet's call, but it never came. They figured she must have either forgotten or was too embarrassed about her behaviour to check in so they waited a couple of days. They hardly went half a week without hearing from the young woman, so they figured she would call soon enough.

On the third day with no call, the Goddard's began to panic, so they decided to visit Kupcinet's West Hollywood apartment to make sure she was okay. What they found shocked them both, and would forever remain in their memories.

Chapter 4

November 30, 1963. West Hollywood. It's been three days since Mark and Marcia sent Karyn Kupcinet home from their dinner party after her strange behaviour. That night, Kupcinet had promised to call the couple the next morning to check in, but she never did. Mark now feared that his good friend had died from a drug overdose.

The couple arrived at Kupcinet's West Hollywood apartment around noon. They walked through the unlocked front door and found a horrific sight—Karyn Kupcinet was lying face-down on the couch. She was completely nude.

The Goddard's immediately contacted the police, who began investigating immediately. Initially, it looked like the Goddard's suspicions had been true, that Kupcinet had overdosed on the number of drugs she had been abusing over the course of the last few years. Investigators found prescriptions and numerous bottles of Desoxyn, Miltown, Amvicel, Thyroid extract and Modaline strewn around Kupcinet's bathroom.

There was other evidence in the apartment that Kupcinet may have taken her own life; the strongest piece of evidence they found to support this was a cryptic note found in her bedroom which reflected her emotions regarding her life, her parents, her self-image, and her boyfriend.

This note was written in a haphazard fashion, a similar style to her diary entries. One of the most poignant pieces of the note read:

I'm no good. I'm not really that pretty. My figure's fat and will never be the way my mother wants it. Why must I be so alone. What's the use of living with nothing to believe it?

Clearly, Kupcinet was not in a good mental state in the months leading up to her death, and this note proved that without a doubt.

Also at the scene, investigators realized that Kupcinet had not died that day. In fact, she had been dead for several days. Her body had begun decomposing and there was evidence that flies had found Kupcinet first, laying eggs in her scalp. None of the eggs had hatched yet.

Additionally, there was some evidence of distress around Kupcinet's living room. The TV was on, but the volume was turned almost all the way down. Nearby the couch was a metal coffee pot and a brandy glass full of cigarette butts that had been overturned on the floor. A coffee cup sat on a side table across a room next to a pile of matches that had been shredded and cut up by scissors.

In Kupcinet's bedroom, investigators found that all of her dresser drawers were opened and most of the contents had been flung across the room.

Because it was clear that Kupcinet's mental health was unstable leading up to her death, police weren't sure if the mess they found in the apartment was a sign that a struggle had occurred or simply another indication of Kupcinet's mental distress. Form the scene alone, they were unable to determine whether Kupcinet had died from an attack, an accident, or an unintentional suicide.

Kupcinet's body was transferred to a nearby coroner. Sidney Korshak, a Los Angeles based lawyer that had been friends with the Kupcinet family for years, officially identified her body the next day. Shortly after Kupcinet was officially identified, an autopsy was performed on her corpse. The results of which shocked everyone in the case.

After the coroner completed the autopsy, it was determined that Karyn Kupcinet had in fact been murdered. According to the coroner, she had been dead for two days, and her cause of death was manual strangulation due to injuries on her neck that included a compression fracture to the left side of her hyoid bone with deep soft tissue hemorrhages in her neck, thyroid gland, and larynx.

After the autopsy, Kupcinet's body was returned to her hometown, Chicago, where she was laid to rest just outside of the city in Skokie, Illinois. While over 500 people attended her funeral, Andrew Prine did not.

After Karyn was laid to rest, the Kupcinet family was ready for investigators to discover who had murdered their beloved daughter so they could begin to heal. They had no idea at the time the media frenzy that would surround their daughter's murder later, or that the mystery of her death would never be officially solved.

Chapter 5

Karyn Kupcinet's death was initially highly publicized in the Los Angeles media, especially when it was discovered that another up-and-coming star was the main suspect—Andrew Prine. The LAPD believed that Prine was one of the only people who would have had a motive to kill Kupcinet. If she died, he would no longer be haunted by his ex-girlfriend who refused to let him forget her. As well, Prine strongly suspected that Kupcinet had been behind the threatening letters that tormented him.

As well, Prine had spoken to Kupcinet over the phone several times the day before she died, arguing, which was overheard by multiple sources. Prine had an airtight alibi for the night that Kupcinet was killed, but his friends, Robert Hathaway and Edward Rubin, had admitted to spending time with Kupcinet the night she was killed. The pair had told police that they left Kupcinet's apartment that night around 11:30p.m., but the only witness who could corroborate this was Andrew Prine himself.

Unfortunately, Prine, Hathaway, and Rubin had all admitted to being in Kupcinet's apartment shortly before her death, police were forced to accredit all physical evidence of them in the apartment to other times. They found no physical evidence that could directly tie either of the three men to Kupcinet at the time of her death.

The LAPD, along with Kupcinet's family, was pretty sure the three men were responsible for Karyn's death, but pretty sure doesn't stand up in a court of law. None of the men ever faced charges in the crime.

With no exciting breaks in the case, Karyn Kupcinet's murder quickly fell out of the newspapers in Los Angeles and out of the minds of its residents. It wasn't until 1967 that Kupcinet's story was thought of by many outside of her own family.

In 1967, Penn Jones Jr., a researcher with a love of conspiracy theories, self-published the book *Forgive My Grief II*, which attempted to present a set of facts as evidence that the JFK assassination hadn't happened the way the media and the government had claimed.

John F. Kennedy was assassinated the day before Kupcinet died. According to Jones, who cited an Associated Press story, an unidentified woman had called her local operator twenty minutes before the assassination of the President, warning of the impending attack. Jones believed that the unidentified woman was Karyn Kupcinet.

Jones cited as proof the fact that the call had come from California, and that Kupcinet's murder could have been connected to her spilling a deadly secret. Karyn, Jones claimed, heard about the assassination from her father, Irv Kupcinet, who allegedly had been told by Jack Ruby, Oswald's killer, whom Irv had met in the 1940s.

Irv Kupcinet continued to deny that he or his daughter had any knowledge of the President's assassination before the rest of America right up until his own death in 2003. Kupcinet wrote about his daughter in *Kup's Column*. In 1992, NBC's *Today Show* ran a segment on mysterious deaths that occurred after JFK's assassination, including Karyn's death. Irv again spoke out against the idea that Karyn had any role in the story surrounding the assassination. He insisted again that both his family and the LAPD knew exactly who had been responsible for her death—Andrew Prine, Robert Hathaway, and Edward Rubin—there just wasn't, nor would there ever be, enough evidence to prove it to a court.

When Irv Kupcinet passed away on November 10, 2003, He was laid to rest next to his daughter and wife, who passed away in 2001. Irv's death marked the end of an era to many Chicagoans, just as it put an end to the investigation into Karyn Kupcinet's death.

In her quest to be seen on every silver screen, Karyn Kupcinet lost sight of herself. Striving to be skinny, the young starlet abused her mind and body excess amounts of prescription and diet pills. When her mind went, so did her chances of finding love and happiness, no matter how hard she tried to maintain it.

Karyn Kupcinet's final appearance on television came a year after her death in 1964. Kupcinet had guest starred on an episode of *Perry Mason*, which had been in post-production at the time of her death and the following year. To many who saw her performance, it seemed the young beauty was just beginning her rise to fame, but she was already gone, taken from the world many years too early.

www.ingramcontent.com/pod-product-compliance
Lightning Source LLC
Chambersburg PA
CBHW031450130726
47989CB00003B/1332